Drinks For All The Family

Published by Octopus Books Limited
59 Grosvenor Street, London W.I
First published 1973
© 1973 Octopus Books Pty Ltd

ISBN 0 7064 0214 6

Produced by Mandarin Publishers Limited
77a Marble Road, North Point, Hong Kong
and printed in Hong Kong

Photography: Norman Nicholls
Design and Illustration: Kit Keane

Drinks For All The Family

Wendy Phippard

Octopus Books

Introduction

Drinks are decorative, easy to prepare and endless in variety. They can make the simplest family meal both festive and more fun, and turn an ordinary party into the most memorable occasion. This book is an informal collection of recipes for all kinds of drinks for all kinds of people.

The instructions are simple, you will not need a great array of ingredients or professional bar instruments for most of the recipes, and you will enjoy experimenting with the new and unusual drink ideas to be found on every page. Unusual ingredients are defined and described in a note below recipes in which they appear.

Food in fluid form, particularly milk and eggs, is easily prepared in a wide variety of ways, and is readily digested, so that liquid meals are ideal for people in a hurry. Other drink recipes help those with time on their hands to relax and unwind.

There are drinks in this book that will appeal to every member of the family at any time of the day, for every mood and occasion: drinks to revive and refresh the tired sportsman; drinks to make a success of every child's party; drinks to cool and revitalize in a hot climate; drinks to carry you right through the day; drinks to stimulate the appetite; and drinks to cure and comfort a variety of ills.

In the pages that follow, you will find suggestions for equipment used to mix both alcoholic and non-alcoholic drinks. Often you can make do without the full kit recommended, and tips are given for substitute equipment.

Many drinks fit into two or more categories. A cool summer drink may be both wine and spirit based, and a hot drink may require blender-mixing. A number of non-alcoholic mixed drinks would be ideal for children's parties, and several cocktails are well-served after dinner with coffee.

Recipes are given with quantities to serve one, unless otherwise specified.

4

Many recipes call for 'lemon or lime juice'. These ingredients are not interchangeable, as use of one or the other gives a different flavour. However, lemon can be substituted for lime, and in Australia this is often necessary, as limes are not commonly available.

SWEETENING DRINKS

Most recipes call for powdered or castor sugar sprinkled over ice, or shaken well with liquid ingredients. The sugar will dissolve quite well, but as there is often some residue, many people prefer to use a sugar syrup. 2 fluid ounces of the syrup given below is equal to 1 ounce by weight of powdered sugar.

4 parts of sugar mixed with 4 parts of water, stirred till liquid boils and all sugar is dissolved.

Fruit syrups are marketed in many flavours. Grenadine is commonly used in mixed drinks and cocktails, and is pomegranate based. Recipes in this book call for citron (lemon), menthe (peppermint) and cassis (blackcurrant). Some recipes, particularly in the non-alcoholic mixed drinks and children's drinks chapters, call for the sweet fruit syrups that are sold in supermarkets and by grocers for flavouring of ice cream, milk shakes and other drinks.

GARNISHES

Maraschino cherries; sprigs of mint; sprigs of celery foliage; slices of lemon, lime and orange; twists of lemon, lime and orange peel; strips of cucumber peel; green olives; chopped or sliced fresh fruit.

SAVOURIES TO SERVE WITH DRINKS

Can be kept simple. It is easiest to serve a platter or two with whole cheeses and savoury crackers; caviar or oysters on the shell, with slices of lemon and thinly sliced brown bread and butter; bowls of peeled prawns; olives.

Terms Used

Angostura bitters: a concentrate of herbs used in very small quantities to flavour both cocktails and mixed drinks, alcoholic and non-alcoholic.

bar spoon: a long-handled spoon.

chilling: for a cold drink, use cold implements and utensils. Chill a shaker by putting ice in it beforehand. When shaker is cool, pour off water and add ingredients. To chill glasses, fill with ice, then empty just before serving drink. Rub inside of glass with a cloth. Extra unwanted water can spoil a drink.

float: to float brandy or other spirits, carefully rest a small spoon, bottom side up, with the handle on the edge of the glass, and the tip of the spoon touching the liquid in the glass. Pour the spirit or liquor over the back of the spoon.

ice: cubes made in a mould,
cracked ice is obtained by roughly breaking cubes
crushed ice is obtained commercially, or can be made in an ice crusher
shaved ice, so fine it can be drunk through a straw, is used in frappés and juleps and can be made in a home ice crusher, or by hammering crushed ice in a strong plastic bag.

measuring: a screwtop spirit measure gives a jigger or 1½ fluid ounces. A dash is 1/6 of a teaspoon. With practice you can judge quantities without a measure, though a pint measure is almost a necessity.

mixing: mix ingredients with a glass rod in a mixing glass then pour over ice in serving glass.

shaking:	to mix ingredients, particularly eggs, liquors, and juices with liquors. Use a professional cocktail shaker, either with wire strainer incorporated in lid, or with a separate bar strainer; or you can get equally good results using a screwtop bottle and a fine mesh strainer.
stirring:	use a glass rod or bar spoon to stir ingredients in glass in which drink is to be served.
sugar-frosted:	glass sprinkled inside with a few pinches icing sugar.
sugar-crusted:	rim of glass dampened and pushed into about ⅛ inch castor (powdered) sugar so that the rim is coated.
vermouth:	recipes calling for sweet vermouth require Italian vermouth; dry vermouth is the French variety.

DRINK MIXING IMPLEMENTS

The essentials are:

a lemon or lime juice squeezer: the small metal device that squeezes a half or quarter lemon for one drink
a conventional orange squeezer
a small sharp knife
a cutting board
a mixing (bar) spoon
a screwtop measure, or a measuring cup for spirits
a corkscrew
a bottle opener

Almost essential:

a cocktail shaker; you can manage quite well with a screwtop bottle and a fine mesh kitchen strainer

Useful:

an ice crusher
an ice bucket
a soda water syphon

Bottled soda water is very acceptable, but more expensive than the refillable syphon kind.

You can keep ice in the refrigerator, but it is more convenient to keep it in an insulated ice bucket wherever you are mixing drinks.

An electric blender: with this machine, there is no end to the fresh and foamy drinks that you will be able to prepare. However, you can often get a satisfactory result with a shaker, or by whisking.

Of course you will need glasses. There are special glasses for almost every drink, but small (5-7 oz) tumblers, large (8-10 oz) tumblers, long glasses (10-12 oz), wine glasses, champagne glasses and large and small cocktail glasses should cover almost all requirements.

Measures

Measures used in this book are fluid ounces and pints.

The Imperial pint, used in all recipes in this book, measures 20 fluid ounces.

Metric measures: for easy reference,

1 litre = 1¾ pints (working equivalent)
½ litre = 1 pint (working equivalent)
½ kilogramme (500 grammes) = 1 lb (working equivalent)

There are recipes given for fresh lemonade, which is sweetened, diluted, fresh lemon juice.

When a recipe calls for fruit or vegetable juice, the fresh variety should be used if available. However unsweetened canned juices are a satisfactory substitute.

Blender Drinks

Some excellent mixed alcoholic drinks can be made in a blender. You will find several of these in this chapter, but I have concentrated on health drinks and 'complete-meal' drinks. For other blender cocktails, see chapters 2 and 4.

An electric blender is a versatile and invaluable aid to making drinks. Fruit and vegetable juices and cocktails are an instant source of natural vitamins and minerals, and taste a lot better than the tinned variety. A quickly mixed egg flip sets you up for the day; or you may enjoy this nourishing snack before a cocktail party.

Some of the drinks in this chapter include brandy or rum as an optional ingredient. The spirit adds flavour, but you may substitute vanilla essence, or leave it out entirely.

Many of these blender drinks can be made in a shaker. They will not be quite as frothy as the blender version, but will be palatable, and just as nutritious.

Vegetables liquidised in a blender may be too fibrous to produce a satisfactory juice. Particularly with crisp vegetables, such as carrots or celery, it may be necessary to use a juice extractor that separates fluid and fibre.

Cool Quencher

Basic Egg Flip

Serves 1

6 fl oz milk
1 egg
1 dessertspoon sugar

To flavour:
1 level tablespoon cocoa mixed to paste with warm water
OR: 1 heaped teaspoon instant coffee dissolved in 1 tablespoon
     warm water.
OR: 1 tablespoon thick fruit flavouring syrup (substitute
     flavouring for sugar)
OR: 1 teaspoon vanilla essence
OR: 1 oz rum, whisky or brandy

Shake, beat or blend thoroughly milk, egg and sugar with chosen
flavouring ingredient.
If using sweet flavouring syrup, omit sugar.

Mediterranean Tomato Juice

Serves 4—6

2 lbs ripe tomatoes
1 small green pepper
1 small onion
1 tablespoon fresh chopped basil
OR: 1 teaspoon dried basil leaves
1 tablespoon Worcestershire sauce
1 large lemon
1 tablespoon olive oil.

Skin tomatoes (first immerse in boiling water and allow to
stand for one minute).
Roughly slice tomatoes. Chop green pepper and onion finely.
Place together with other ingredients in liquidiser, and blend
thoroughly.
Strain or sieve.
Serve chilled.

Sweet Treat

Serves 6

1 pint milk
8 tablespoons finely chopped glace or dried fruit
1 oz castor sugar
2 fl oz Grand Marnier (optional)
¼ pint cream

Blend or thoroughly shake milk, fruit, sugar and liqueur.
Pour into small tumblers and top with lightly whipped cream.

Cool Quencher

Serves 4

1 large cucumber
1 medium avocado pear
5 tablespoons chopped parsley
juice one large lemon
1 tablespoon olive oil
16 fl oz crushed ice
cucumber peel and lemon slices to garnish

Peel and roughly chop cucumber. Peel avocado and cut flesh
from stone.
Blend all ingredients in liquidiser until ice is melted.
Strain into glasses, and serve garnished with cucumber peel and
lemon slices.

Strawberry Whip

Serves 4

1½ pints milk
1 lb strawberries
4 generously piled tablespoons ice cream
2 oz sugar or more to taste
1 teaspoon vanilla
OR
1 tablespoon brandy
ice cubes
3 oz cream, lightly whipped
strawberries to garnish

Blend first five ingredients in blender.
Pour onto ice cube in tall glass.
Top with generous swirl whipped cream and one or two whole strawberries.
To make this drink without a liquidiser:
Puree strawberries by pushing through a fine mesh sieve or strainer.
Put five ingredients together in a bowl and beat thoroughly with an egg beater.
Serve as above.

Cherry Flip

Serves 3

½ pint milk
8 fl oz cherry pulp
1 egg
2 crushed yeast tablets
chopped nuts for garnish

Shake or blend milk, cherry pulp, egg and powdered yeast tablets.
Pour into glasses and top with chopped nuts.
Note: Use canned or stewed cherries. Pulp fruit with juice.

Chocoffee

Serves 1

1 heaped teaspoon cocoa
1 teaspoon instant coffee
1 tablespoon sugar
½ pint milk
1 tablespoon ice cream
cinnamon

Mix cocoa, coffee and sugar to a paste with a spoonful of milk.
Add the rest of the milk.
Shake or beat vigorously or blend in liquidiser.
Top with ice cream and sprinkle with cinnamon.

Eggs and Coffee

Serves 3—4

1 raw egg
2 dessertspoons castor sugar
1 dessertspoon white rum or brandy (optional)
½ teaspoon vanilla essence
1 pint strong coffee
ice cubes

Blend first five ingredients in liquidiser, or beat until frothy.
Pour onto ice cubes in squat 6-8 oz. glasses.

Hyannis Apple Drink

Serves 2

1 apple
1 tablespoon ground almonds
1 tablespoon honey
12 fl oz milk
chopped almonds to decorate

Peel and chop apple. Liquidise in blender.
Add almonds, honey and milk and blend.
It may be necessary to thin honey with a little hot water.
Serve topped with chopped almonds.
Note: If you don't have a blender, stew apple to a pulp with
3 oz water. Strain apple pulp and shake thoroughly with
ground almonds, honey and milk.

Banana Cream

Serves 2

15 fl oz milk
1 dessertspoon brewer's yeast
1 tablespoon honey
1 dessertspoon powdered milk
1 banana (roughly chopped)
1 egg

Blend all ingredients in liquidiser.
To make this drink without a liquidiser:
Purée banana by pushing through a mesh strainer. Put all
ingredients together in a bowl and beat thoroughly.

Peach Froth

Serves 2

8 fl oz stewed peach juice
6 fl oz milk
1 teaspoon honey
1 egg white
ground nutmeg to garnish

Blend or vigorously beat juice, milk, honey and egg white.
Serve chilled, sprinkled with nutmeg.

To make stewed peach juice:
1 ripe peach, mashed or minced
2 oz sugar
6 fl oz water

Simmer ingredients for 45 minutes.
Cool and strain.
Note : It may be convenient to make a larger quantity and keep
refrigerated.

Fruity Milk

Serves 2

8 fl oz soft fruit pulp (berries, apricots, bananas)
8 fl oz milk

To pulp fruit:
1. Mince, mash or sieve canned fruit with juice
2. Simmer ½ lb fruit with 2 oz sugar and 2 fl oz water until pulpy.

Blend or shake fruit pulp with milk.
Note: Keep a large quantity of fruit pulp in the refrigerator and mix this nourishing drink for breakfast or for children after school.

Mandarin Milkshake

Serves 2—3

1 x 8 oz can mandarin segments
OR: 2 small mandarins
    1 oz sugar
    4 fl oz water
½ pint milk
½ teaspoon ground ginger
crystallized ginger to decorate

Mash, liquidise or sieve canned mandarin fruit and juice, removing any membranes.
If using fresh fruit, peel and segment the mandarins, cover with sugar and water and simmer 5 minutes.
Shake or blend mandarin liquid with milk and ground ginger.
Pour into glasses and top with finely chopped crystallized ginger.

Fruit Refresher

Serves 4

½ pint unsweetened pineapple juice
½ pint fresh orange juice
½ pint unsweetened grapefruit juice
1 tablespoon finely chopped mint
crushed ice

Mix juices with chopped mint in a large jug or bowl.
To serve, quarter fill tall glasses with crushed ice and fill with
juice mixture.
Note: Use freshly squeezed or separated juice if available.

Passionfruit Punch

Serves 2 — 3

8 fl oz apricot juice
4 fl oz water
1 dessertspoon honey
1 mashed banana
pulp of 3 passionfruit
1 tablespoon lemon juice

Mix lukewarm water with honey and mix in with mashed
banana.
Sieve banana liquid, add remaining ingredients and shake
thoroughly.
Note: If you use a liquidiser, blend all ingredients together.
It will not be necessary to purée banana separately.

BOOZE

NAN BREAD / CHAPATIS / VEG... IR

PLATES.

GLASSES. } crockery.

CUTLERY.

INVITATIONS

~~TABLE~~ ~~CLOTHS~~

HOT PLATE.

NAPKINS.

TORCHES.

HEATERS.

W/W Punch.. etc.

Garden Cocktail

Serves 3 — 4

½ lb carrots
2 large apples
3 sticks celery
ground pepper
crushed walnuts to garnish

Peel apples and carrots.
Chop carrots and apples into ¼ inch to ½ inch cubes.
Finely slice celery
Place chopped apples and vegetables in liquidiser to blend.
Add pepper to taste.
Pour into glasses and garnish with chopped walnuts.
Note: You will need a powerful liquidiser to mix this properly.
If carrots are very crisp, a juice extractor may be required.
Alternatively: blend ingredients in liquidiser, substituting
canned or home-made carrot juice for whole carrots.

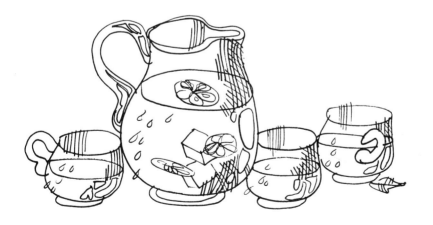

Long, Cool Drinks Spirit - Based

This chapter contains recipes for individual drinks and for party quantities.

Try substituting spirits other than those specified for further variety. For example, the gin sling and the gin fizz could be made with brandy, whisky, rum or applejack (apple brandy); the Collins can be made with rum, brandy, applejack or gin; the cobbler is excellent with rum or whisky.

Some of these recipes, such as Fresh Egg Lemonade and Brandy Egg Sour, call for a whole raw egg. These are nourishing drinks, and after a late breakfast, they could well take the place of a lunch-time snack.

Many of the drinks in this chapter can be served before dinner as an alternative to the shorter cocktail. Others, particularly the punches, are designed especially for drinking at parties and with casual outdoor meals.

Rum Tea

Serves approx. 36

½ lb. sugar
1 pint water
4 pints strong black tea
½ pint lemon juice
rind of one lemon, cut into thin strips
1 bottle apple brandy (applejack) or calvados
1 bottle dark rum
1 bottle claret
handful of mint sprigs to garnish

Boil sugar and water till dissolved.
Mix tea, sugar syrup and lemon juice, pour over large block of
ice in a punch bowl.
Add lemon rind, spirits and wine and stir.
Garnish with mint sprigs.

Whisky Cola

2 fl oz Scotch whisky
½ fl oz curaçao
½ fl oz lemon juice
2 dashes Angostura bitters
crushed ice
cola
twist of orange peel to garnish

Mix whisky, curaçao, lemon juice and Angostura bitters in a glass.
Add a heaped spoon of crushed ice, and fill with cola.
Garnish with orange peel and serve with a swizzle stick.

Apricot Cooler

crushed ice
1 stewed or canned apricot
1½ fl oz apricot brandy
½ fl oz lemon juice
1 teaspoon icing sugar

Pack an 8-10 oz glass two-thirds full with crushed ice.
Roughly sieve the apricot and mash well with a fork.
Shake apricot pulp with apricot brandy, lemon juice and icing sugar.
Add ice to shaker, shake again, and pour whole drink, unstrained, back into glasses.

Orange Julep

Serves approx. 16

crushed ice
2 oz icing sugar
13 fl oz brandy
1 pint 6 fl oz claret
3 fl oz cointreau
1 pint fresh orange juice
1 pint unsweetened pineapple juice
mint sprigs and orange slices to garnish

Half-fill a five pint capacity jug or punch bowl with
crushed ice.
Sprinkle sugar over ice.
Add first five ingredients, stir gently.
Garnish with mint sprigs and orange rings.
Fill glasses from jug or bowl as required.

Harvey Wallbanger

1 fl oz vodka
½ fl oz galliano liqueur
6 fl oz orange juice

Mix all ingredients together in a tumbler and add ice cube.

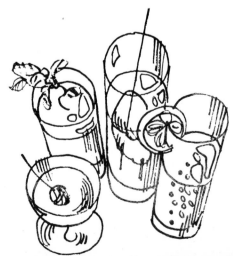

Rum Punch

Serves 8

2 tablespoons honey
2 tablespoons warm water
juice of 4 large lemons
½ pint white rum
5 tablespoons roughly chopped or torn mint leaves
1 level tablespoon tea
2 pints boiling water
1 pint 6 fl oz dry ginger ale
ice cubes

Dissolve honey in warm water.
Put liquid honey, lemon juice and rum together in tall jug. Add
mint leaves and leave to stand while brewing tea.
Pour boiling water onto tea leaves and allow to stand 5 minutes.
Strain tea off leaves and chill tea.
Pour chilled tea and dry ginger ale into rum mixture. Stir well.
To serve: pour over one ice cube in each glass.

Pimms Cup

2 fl oz pimms
2 fl oz rye whisky
lemonade
slice cucumber, orange and lemon peel and cherry
for decoration

Pour whisky into a tall glass and mix in pimms. Top with lemonade.
Decorate with cucumber peel and lemon peel and with a
cocktail stick attach cherry to orange peel.
Add ice and serve immediately

Rye Rickey

1 fl oz rye whisky
juice of half a lemon or lime
cube of ice
a long strip of lemon or lime peel
soda

Put rye whisky with lemon or lime juice into bottom of a
5-7 fl oz tumbler.
Add ice cube and twist of peel.
Fill with soda.
Alternative: Use rum, gin or applejack; the lemon or lime
juice, ice, peel and soda complete the traditional ' rickey '.

Bacardi Cup

½ bottle Bacardi
6 fl oz Pineapple Juice
juice of 12 oranges
juice of 6 lemons
dash of Angostura bitters
mint sprigs, orange and lemon slices for decoration

Fill a punch bowl, previously lined with crushed ice,
with chilled wine, orange and lemon juice.
Add Angostura bitters and stir thoroughly.
Garnish with mint sprigs and orange and lemon slices.

Brandied Orange Champagne

Serves 8

½ pint brandy
1 fl oz cointreau
½ fl oz Angostura bitters
1 bottle champagne
crushed ice

Mix brandy, cointreau and bitters in a jug.
Half-fill sugar-frosted tumblers (8-10 fl oz capacity) with
crushed ice.
Add 1½ fl oz brandy mixture and fill with champagne.

Pernod Fizz

1 fl oz pernod
juice of half lemon
½ fl oz grenadine
dash of dark rum
4 fl ozs champagne

Mix pernod, lemon juice, grenadine and rum in a tall glass,
8-10 fl oz capacity.
Add an ice cube and fill with champagne.

Dubonnet Lemon Cup

2 fl oz Dubonnet
Juice of 3 lemons
soda or mineral water
grated nutmeg to garnish
crushed ice

Pour Dubonnet with crushed ice into a tall glass and then
add lemon juice.
Top with soda or mineral water and garnish with
grated nutmeg.

Brandied Milk Punch

16 fl oz chilled milk
2-3 strips orange rind
6 tablespoons Brandy
2 teaspoons castor sugar
crushed ice
½ teaspoon nutmeg

Steep orange rind in brandy for 1 hour.
Pour brandy and orange rind into chilled milk, add nutmeg
and blend or beat until frothy.
Pour into tall, chilled glasses and dust with nutmeg.

Shandy Gaff

4 fl oz chilled beer
4 fl oz chilled ginger ale

Pour beer and ginger ale into a tall, chilled glass.
Stir briefly with tall spoon and serve — without ice.

Rum Knockout

1 fl oz White Rum
1 fl oz pineapple juice
1 fl oz grapefruit juice
3 dashes white curaçao

Shake all ingredients together and strain into a tumbler or
tall glass.

Gin Cooler

2 fl oz Gin
1 fl oz lemon juice
creme de menthe
1 dash angostura bitters
1 egg white, beaten

Shake all ingredients together and pour into a tall glass.
Add crushed ice and serve.

Livornese

2 fl oz campari
1 fl oz grappa
2 fl oz curaçao

Shake all ingredients together and serve in a cocktail tumbler.
No ice.

Fresh Egg Lemonade

Serves 1

1 raw egg
2 fl oz lemon juice
1½ fl oz brandy
1 teaspoon castor sugar
soda water
ice cube

Blend or shake first five ingredients.
Strain into 8-10 fl oz glass.
Fill with chilled soda.
Top with an ice cube.

Rum and Coke Sour

crushed ice
1 fl oz lemon juice
2 fl oz white rum
cola

Quarter fill tall glass with crushed ice.
Add lemon juice and rum, fill with cola and serve with a
swizzle stick.

Apple Power

Serves 4

4 fl oz apple brandy (applejack) or calvados
½ pint sweet apple cider
2 fl oz grand marnier
¼ teaspoon ground cloves
¼ teaspoon ground cinnamon
2 cups crushed ice

Blend all ingredients in a liquidiser.
Pour unstrained into tall glasses.
Note: If you do not have an electric blender, shake very
thoroughly, allow to stand several minutes, then shake again
before pouring unstrained into glasses.

Brandy Egg Sour

1½ fl oz brandy
1½ fl oz curacao
1 fl oz lemon juice
1 egg
1 teaspoon castor sugar
½ cup finely crushed ice

Shake all ingredients together thoroughly.
Strain into large tumbler.

Brandy Cobbler

2 fl oz brandy
1 teaspoon sugar
1 cup crushed ice
a finger pineapple and 2 slices orange,
OR: strawberries and 2 slices peach
soda

Stir sugar and brandy until sugar is well dissolved.
Pour sweetened brandy over crushed ice in a large tumbler.
Add fruit and fill with soda.

Iced Irish Coffee

½ pint strong, iced and sweetened black coffee
2 fl oz Irish whisky
crushed ice
whipped cream

Mix whisky and coffee in a tall glass and add ice.
Decorate with whipped cream and serve.

Gin Fizz

½ fl oz gin
½ fl oz dry vermouth
juice of half lemon or lime
2 fl oz dry white wine
ice cube
soda

Mix gin, vermouth, lemon or lime juice and wine in a tall glass.
Add one large ice cube and fill glass with soda.

Whisky Collins

1 fl oz rye whisky
½ teaspoon icing sugar
juice of half a lemon
crushed ice
soda water
lemon peel to garnish

Shake whisky, sugar and lemon juice with crushed ice.
Strain into 8-20 fl oz glass and fill with soda water.
Garnish with a twist of lemon peel.

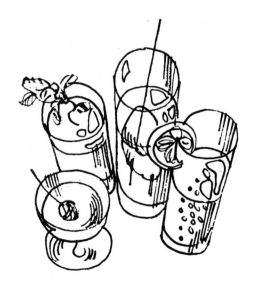

Mint Julep

1 teaspoon castor sugar
8 small mint leaves
2 fl oz rye whisky
soda
2 mint sprigs to garnish

Crush sugar and mint leaves with the back of a spoon.
Add a splash of soda to dissolve sugar, then add whisky.
Mix well then strain over crushed ice in a 6-8 fl oz. tumbler.
Garnish with sprigs of mint.
Alternative: Use gin, brandy, rum or bourbon.

Coffee Ice

Serves 2—3

½ pint vanilla ice cream
2 fl oz Tia Maria
2 fl oz brandy

Blend ingredients in liquidiser till smooth.
Serve in tumblers with long-handled spoon.

Golden Tonic

½ fl oz galliano
1½ fl oz advocaat
1 fl oz vodka
½ fl oz lemon juice
tonic water
ice cube

Mix liqueurs, vodka, and lemon juice in 8-10 fl oz glass.
Fill glass with chilled tonic and add an ice cube.
Note: Galliano is a golden-coloured, liquorice flavoured liqueur.
Advocaat is a thick, yellow liqueur, made of egg yolks and
brandy. Like galliano, it is a smooth mixer.

Vodka Cup

10 oz berry fruit, raspberries or cranberries
3 bananas, diced
1 lb chopped pineapple
1 x 26 fl oz bottle lemonade
1 pint vodka

Mix berry fruit with bananas, pineapple and lemonade.
Chill well, overnight if possible.
Place ¼ cup fruit mixture in each tall glass. Add ice cubes and
top glass with vodka.
Serve immediately with a tall spoon.

Palm Beach

1 fl oz gin
2 fl oz grapefruit juice
Champagne
crushed ice

Mix gin, grapefruit juice and ice together in a tall glass.
Top with champagne. No decoration.

Gin Sling

2 fl oz gin
1 fl oz port
dry ginger ale
dash of orange bitters
twist of orange peel to garnish

Pour gin and port over ice cube in 8-10 fl oz glass. Mix.
Fill with dry ginger ale.
Add a dash of bitters and garnish with orange peel.

Lemon Cloud

1 fl oz vodka
1 fl oz pernod
juice of half a lemon
coca cola
ice cube

Pour vodka, pernod and lemon juice into tall glass.
Fill with coca cola, and top with an ice cube to serve.
Note: Pernod is aniseed-flavoured, and turns cloudy when
mixed with water or other ingredients.

Long, Cool Drinks Wine-Based

Most of the recipes in this chapter are for summer party punches and cups.

Some contain spirits, brandy or rum, and quite a number make use of fortified wines such as port, sherry, vermouth and marsala.

Apart from these stronger mixtures, most of the recipes simply combine table wines with fruit juices, tea, soft drinks and flavouring agents. These light refreshing punches are perfect for sipping through a long hot day, at home, at the beach or by a pool, or for serving in more copious quantities at a summer evening party.

A punch bowl can be decorated with flowers and fruits, and provides a special feature on a sideboard or buffet table.

Port Flip

Serves 2

4 fl oz port
1 egg
1 teaspoon castor sugar
1 fl oz benedictine
1 cup crushed ice
nutmeg

Blend port, egg, benedictine, sugar and ice in liquidiser.
Pour unstrained into glasses and serve sprinkled with nutmeg.

Sangria

Serves 12—15

There are many versions of this refreshing drink of the
Mediterranean. Here is a typical recipe:

2 bottles dry red wine
½ bottle brandy
1 teaspoon orange bitters
1½ pints soda
cucumber fingers, strips of cucumber peel, orange slices and
    mint sprigs to garnish

Mix wine, brandy and bitters in a punch bowl.
Add a large block of ice, and pour in soda.
Garnish with cucumber, orange and mint.

Orange Vermouth

Serves 12 – 15

1 bottle dry vermouth
½ bottle curaçao
1 pint orange juice
crushed ice
soda
cucumber peel

Mix vermouth, curaçao and orange juice in jug with several handfuls of crushed ice.
Half-fill ½ pint glasses with orange mixture and fill with soda.

Fruit Float

Serves 24–30

approx 1½ lb chopped fruit (pineapple, oranges, peaches, apricots,
    strawberries)
1 bottle brandy or rum
8 oz sugar
3 bottles dry white wine
fresh fruit to garnish
soda (optional)

Soak fruit, sugar and brandy or rum overnight.
Place in a punch bowl with a large block of ice.
Pour in white wine and garnish with fresh fruit.
Serve straight, or pour into glasses and top with soda to taste.

Peaches 'n Pineapple

Serves approx. 18

1 pineapple
8 peaches
1 bottle dry white wine
1 bottle champagne
crushed ice
peach slices to garnish

Peel pineapple, slice and chop roughly, discarding hard core.
Peel and slice peaches. Place pineapple and peach pieces
together in liquidiser and blend. Pour fruit purée into punch
bowl or large jug. Add white wine and champagne. Stir gently.
Add approximately 2 pints of crushed ice. Use any liquid
measure to determine quantity.
Garnish with peach slices.
Serve in individual punch cups, tumblers or wine glasses.

Pink Pear

Serves 10 — 12

1 pear
1 lemon
2 oz sugar
8 fl oz water
4 cloves
1 bottle rosé wine
½ bottle port
crushed ice
soda
fresh pear slices to garnish

Peel and slice pear. Carefully cut peel in strips from lemon,
leaving pith and segments intact.
Put pear slices, lemon peel, sugar, water and cloves together in
saucepan, simmer with lid on until fruit is quite soft and pulpy.
Remove cloves and lemon rind. Allow to cool and sieve fruit
with juice.
Mix rosé wine, port and pear pulp with the juice of the lemon
and several handfuls of crushed ice in a tall jug.
Garnish with fresh pear slices and serve in glasses with soda to
taste.

Wine Cup

Serves 24–30

1 bottle dry sherry
1 bottle brandy
1 bottle white dessert wine
2 bottles sparkling/dry white wine, preferably champagne
strawberries (optional)

Mix sherry, brandy and dessert wine in punch bowl.
Add a large block of ice.
Pour in champagne and garnish with fruit if required.
Serve in large champagne glasses.

Spritzer

4 fl oz medium dry white wine
soda

Half-fill a tall glass with a moselle-type white wine.
Fill with soda and top with an ice cube.

Sweet Red

2 fl oz sweet vermouth
1 fl oz campari
juice of half a lemon
ice cubes
twist of lemon peel
soda

Mix vermouth, campari and lemon juice in a tall glass.
Add ice cubes and twist of peel.
Fill with soda and serve.

Sherry Sangaree

½ teaspoon castor sugar
2 fl oz medium dry sherry
sprinkle nutmeg
slice of lemon or lime

Mix sugar, sherry and nutmeg until sugar is almost dissolved.
Pour sherry mixture over ice cubes in a small tumbler.
Garnish with slice of lemon and serve.

Pink Pear and
Peaches 'n Pineapple

Summer Sauterne

Serves 16 — 20

2 bottles sauterne (or other white dessert wine)
8 fl oz cointreau
8 fl oz brandy
juice of 2 lemons
2 x 26 fl oz bottles tonic water
orange and lemon slices and mint to garnish
crushed ice

Mix sauterne, cointreau, brandy and lemon juice in a punch
bowl.
Add several handfuls of crushed ice, and pour in tonic water.
Serve in tall glasses garnished with a sprig of mint and a slice
each of orange and lemon.

Red Wine Punch

Serves 15—18

2 bottles dry red wine
6 fl ozs port
8 fl ozs cherry brandy
2 fl ozs maraschino liqueur
½ pint orange juice
½ pint grapefruit juice
slices orange and lemon to garnish
15 maraschino cherries to garnish
soda (optional)

Mix all liquid ingredients in punch bowl.
Add large block of ice and garnish with fruit slices and
cherries.
Serve straight, or pour into glasses and top with soda water
to taste.

Dubonnet Champagne

1 lump sugar
2 dashes bitters
1 tablespoon orange juice
½ fl oz dubonnet
1 tablespoon crushed ice
champagne

Place lump sugar in large champagne glass.
Sprinkle with bitters, add orange juice and dubonnet.
Stir till sugar is dissolved.
Add ice and fill glass with champagne.

Marsala Punch

Serves 12—15

12 fl oz marsala
6 fl oz maraschino liqueur
1 pint strong tea
2 large bottles(2½ pints)dry ginger ale
maraschino cherries to garnish

Mix marsala, maraschino and tea in a punch bowl.
Add a large block of ice, pour in dry ginger and garnish with
cherries.

Blackcurrant Vermouth

1½ fl ozs dry vermouth
1½ fl ozs sweet vermouth
1 fl oz creme de cassis
juice of half lemon
soda and ice cubes

Mix vermouths, liqueur and lemon juicee in a tall glass.
Add 2 or 3 ice cubes and fill with soda water.
Note: Creme de cassis is a blackcurrant liqueur.

White Wine Punch

Serves 10 — 12

½ pound cherries, pitted
1 lb fresh pineapple cubes, ¼ inch to ½ inch
4 fl oz kirsch
2 oz castor sugar
1 bottle dry white wine
6 dashes Angostura bitters
1 pint fresh or canned unsweetened pineapple juice
crushed ice.

Marinate cherries and pineapple in kirsch and sugar overnight.
Strain marinade, reserving both fruit and liquid.
Mix wine, bitters, kirsch liquid and pineapple juice in a punch
bowl or large jug.
Add several handfuls of crushed ice and top with reserved fruit.
Serve in 8 oz glasses, about two-thirds punch mixture, filled
with soda.
Note: If fresh pineapple unavailable, use canned fruit. Do not
use juice, and omit sugar from kirsch marinade.

Claret Cup

1 bottle claret
1 bottle sherry
orange bitters
1 x 26 fl oz bottle lemonade
ice cubes
orange and peach slices to garnish

Mix claret, sherry and bitters in a tall jug.
Add lemonade and ice cubes.
Serve in large wine goblets, garnished with slices of orange and
peach.

Champagne Julep

lump sugar
crushed ice
mint sprigs
1 bottle champagne
strawberries to garnish

Put 1 tablespoon crushed ice into each 4 fl oz wine glass with
1 sugar lump.
Add 2 crushed or bruised sprigs of mint to each glass.
Fill with champagne and top with 2 or 3 strawberries or other
fruit in season.

Peach Champagne Cup

Serves 30—36

6 whole peaches
1 pint water
1 lb sugar
1 bottle brandy
3 bottles champagne
6 cups crushed ice

Peel peaches.
Simmer whole peaches in sugar and water until cooked but
still firm.
Cool in syrup and add brandy. Leave to soak overnight.
Put brandy syrup into large punch bowl with crushed ice.
Add champagne.
Slice brandied peaches and add to punch bowl to garnish.
Serve in large champagne glasses.

Cocktails

A cocktail can be defined as any drink served before lunch or dinner, but traditionally it is a short, chilled drink, served in a small, open, stemmed glass, and designed to whet the appetite prior to a meal. Most often it is spirit-based, mixed with vermouth, bitters or some other mixers and flavouring agents.

There are many drinks that fit into the before-dinner category, but that can be enjoyed at any time, and are not so heavily laced with spirits that they cannot safely be drunk through an afternoon. Many of these drinks are broken down with soda or carbonated waters, or by pouring spirits over crushed ice. You will find recipes for these 'cocktails' in chapter 2.

For the sake of classification, this chapter is devoted to the short cocktail drink, about two ounces of ingredients shaken or stirred with ice, strained and poured into a standard three fluid ounce cocktail glass. Some recipes, for example those using champagne or fruit juice, and those that include cream or egg, may require a larger glass, and in these cases the glass size is specified.

Cocktail Equipment

Whisky Sour

1½ fl oz whisky
juice of 1 small lemon
1 teaspoon castor sugar

Shake well with crushed ice and strain into cocktail glass.

Margarita

½ fl oz lime juice
½ fl oz cointreau
1 fl oz tequila
twist of lemon peel to garnish

Shake well with crushed ice and strain into glass.
Traditionally, a margarita is served in a cocktail glass with a
salt-encrusted rim.
Garnish with a twist of lemon peel.
Alternative: Use white rum instead of tequila, and lemon juice
instead of lime juice. In this case, the glass should not be
salt-encrusted.
Note: Tequila is a particularly fiery spirit distilled originally by
Mexican Indians from a type of cactus plant.

Whisky Modern

1 fl oz Scotch whisky
½ fl oz dark rum
½ fl oz pernod
squeeze lemon juice
dash orange bitters

Stir well with ice and strain into cocktail glass.
Note: Pernod is an aniseed-flavoured spirit that turns cloudy
when mixed with water or other liquids.

Delmonico

¾ fl oz gin
½ fl oz dry vermouth
½ fl oz sweet vermouth
½ fl oz cognac
2 dashes Angostura bitters

Pour all ingredients over ice in glass. Stir gently.

Orange Gin

2/3 fl oz fresh orange juice
2/3 fl oz dry gin
2/3 fl oz grand marnier
twist orange peel to garnish

Shake with crushed ice.
Strain into glass and serve garnished with a twist of orange peel.

White Lady

½ fl oz lemon juice
½ fl oz curaçao
1 fl oz dry gin

Shake with crushed ice and strain into cocktail glass.

Vodka and Orange

1 1/3 fl oz orange juice
2/3 fl oz vodka

Shake well with crushed ice and strain into cocktail glass.

Scotch Citrus

1 fl oz Scotch whisky
¾ fl oz grapefruit juice
½ fl oz sweet vermouth
½ fl oz triple sec

Shake all ingredients with crushed ice and strain into large
cocktail glasses.
Note: Triple sec is a colourless, orange-flavoured liqueur.

Black Russian

1 fl oz kahlua (coffee liqueur)
2 fl oz vodka

Pour both kahlua and vodka into tumbler. Add ice cube
and stir.

Gimlet

2 fl oz gin
¼ fl oz triple sec
juice of ½ lime
crushed ice

Combine all ingredients in cocktail shaker and shake
thoroughly. Strain into cocktail glass.

Manhattan

1¹/₃ fl oz Scotch or rye whisky
²/₃ fl oz dry vermouth
1 dash Angostura bitters
a cherry and a twist of lemon peel to garnish

Stir whisky, vermouth and bitters with crushed ice in a mixing
glass.
Strain to serve and garnish with a floating cherry and lemon
peel twist.
Variation: Substitute ¹/₃ fl oz each dry and sweet vermouth for
²/₃ fl oz dry vermouth.

Bloody Mary

1 fl oz vodka
2 fl oz tomato juice
juice of half a lemon
1 dash Worcestershire sauce
freshly ground pepper
a pinch of salt
crushed ice

Shake with crushed ice and strain into glass.
You can produce a satisfactory cocktail by simply stirring
ingredients together. Do not serve till ice is melted.

The traditional Bloody Mary can be made with a few added
ingredients and a little extra style if you have an electric
blender. To serve 3:

3 fl oz vodka
7 fl oz tomato juice
juice of one large lemon
1 egg white
freshly ground pepper
2 large pinches salt
1 teaspoon chopped celery leaves
(you may substitute celery salt for salt and celery leaves)
3 dashes Worcestershire sauce
about 1 cup crushed ice

Blend until ice has melted.

Daiquiri

1^1/$_3$ fl oz white rum
$_2$/$_3$ fl oz lemon juice
^{1}/$_3$ fl oz grenadine

Shake ingredients with crushed ice.
Strain into cocktail glass.

Rusty Nail

1 fl oz Scotch whisky
1 fl oz Drambuie
Lemon peel

Pour all the ingredients into a tumbler, add ice cube
and stir.

Cherry Vodka

1 fl oz vodka
½ fl oz cherry brandy
1 fl oz lemon juice
a cherry and a twist of lemon peel to garnish

Shake vodka, cherry brandy and lemon juice with crushed ice.
Strain into cocktail glass and garnish with cherry and twist of
lemon peel.

Oporto

2/3 fl oz port
2/3 fl oz cointreau
2/3 fl oz orange juice
dash Angostura bitters
twist of orange peel to garnish

Shake port, cointreau, orange juice and bitters with crushed ice.
Strain into cocktail glass and serve garnished with a twist of
orange peel.

Old Fashioned

lump sugar
dash Angostura bitters
soda water
2 fl oz bourbon
ice cubes
slice of orange to garnish

Drop bitters onto sugar lump, then splash with soda to dissolve.
Add whisky and ice cube.
Serve with orange slice in small tumblers.

Martini

1 fl oz dry gin
1 fl oz dry vermouth

Mixed in a cocktail glass and garnished with a twist of lemon peel and an olive, this makes the basic martini.

For a dry martini:
1½ fl oz dry gin
½ fl oz dry vermouth

Mix and serve as above.
Note: Some dry martini drinkers insist that the glass be simply rinsed with vermouth, then filled with gin.

For a sweet martini:
1 fl oz dry gin
1 fl oz sweet vermouth

Mix and serve as for basic martini.

Gin Twist

1 fl oz gin
1 fl oz dubonnet
1/3 fl oz pernod
1 dash orange bitters
lemon peel to garnish

Stir gin, dubonnet, pernod and bitters with ice and strain into large cocktail glass.
Serve garnished with a twist of lemon peel.

Orange Indies

2/3 fl oz dark rum
2/3 fl oz dubonnet
2/3 fl oz orange juice

Shake well with crushed ice and strain into cocktail glass.

Cherry Gin

1 fl oz dry gin
1 fl oz cherry brandy
1 teaspoon maraschino cherry syrup
½ fl oz lemon juice
2 maraschino cherries to garnish

Stir liquid ingredients with ice.
Strain into large cocktail glass and garnish with cherries.

Southern Punch

2/3 fl oz white rum
2/3 fl oz brandy
2/3 fl oz grapefruit juice
dash orange bitters

Shake well with ice and strain into cocktail glass.

Rum Shake

1 fl oz white rum
½ fl oz pernod
½ fl oz pineapple juice
1 dash grenadine
1 teaspoon castor sugar

Shake very thoroughly with castor sugar and strain into
cocktail glass.

Negroni

1 fl oz sweet vermouth
1 fl oz campari bitters,
1 fl oz gin
soda water
lemon peel and orange slice for decoration

Into a tumbler pour sweet vermouth, campari bitters
and gin.
Add ice cube, top with soda water and decorate with
lemon peel and orange slice.

Planters Punch

Serves 3 — 4

4 fl oz dark rum
2 fl oz lime juice
2 fl oz pineapple juice
2 fl oz water
2 dashes grenadine
2 teaspoons brown sugar
cherries and mint leaves to garnish

Shake with crushed ice, strain, and serve in small tumblers or
large cocktail glasses garnished with mint leaves and cherries.

Frappé Mocca

½ cup finely crushed ice
1½ fl oz tia maria or kahlua

Shake very thoroughly and strain into cocktail glass.
Alternatively: Half-fill large cocktail glass with packed ice.
Pour 2 fl oz coffee liqueur over ice and serve with a straw.
Note: Frappes may be made with any liqueur.
Crushed ice and liqueur may be mixed together in an electric
blender and poured straight into large cocktail glasses.
Tia maria and kahlua are both coffee-flavoured liqueurs.

Rob Roy

2 fl oz scotch whisky
¾ fl oz sweet or dry vermouth
maraschino cherry or lemon peel for decoration

Combine all ingredients, stir with ice and strain into
cocktail glass. Decorate with maraschino cherry or
lemon peel.

Over the Rainbow

¹/₃ fl oz creme de menthe
¹/₃ fl oz yellow chartreuse
¹/₃ fl oz grenadine
¹/₃ fl oz green chartreuse
¹/₃ fl oz creme de cacao
¹/₃ fl oz maraschino
¹/₃ fl oz creme de violette
¹/₃ fl oz benedictine
¹/₃ fl oz cognac

Pour liqueurs carefully over the back of a spoon, in layers on top of one another so that the colours do not mix.
You may increase quantities and use fewer ingredients or substitute some other liqueurs such as creme de cassis or Calvados.
Note: This is definitely an after dinner drink. For a pre-dinner cocktail, try using ½ fl oz each of yellow chartreuse, grenadine, brandy and creme de menthe.

Grasshopper

1 fl oz white creme de cacao
1 fl oz green creme de menthe
¾ fl oz cream

Shake all ingredients together with ice and strain into cocktail glass.

B & B

½ fl oz benedictine
½ fl brandy

Mix together and serve in tumbler. No ice.

Golden Shake

1 fl oz advocaat
1 fl oz grapefruit juice
½ egg white

Shake very thoroughly with crushed ice and strain into cocktail glass.

Champagne Julep and
Claret Cup

Sidecar

²/₃ fl oz brandy
²/₃ fl oz cointreau
²/₃ fl oz lemon or lime juice

Shake thoroughly with crushed ice.
Strain into cocktail glass.

Brandy Stinger

1¹/₃ fl oz brandy
²/₃ fl oz white creme de menthe

Stir or shake with crushed ice.
Strain into cocktail glass.

Apricot Curl

²/₃ fl oz brandy
²/₃ fl oz dry vermouth
²/₃ fl oz apricot brandy
twist orange peel

Stir in tall mixing glass with crushed ice.
Strain and serve with twist of orange peel.

Gibson

2 fl oz gin
¾ fl oz dry vermouth
small pickled onion for decoration.

Mix all ingredients together. Add ice cube and decorate
with pickled onion.

Shirley Temple

5 dashes grenadine
maraschino cherry and orange slice for decoration

Pour grenadine into champagne glass with ice cube. Decorate
with maraschino cherry and orange slice.

Brandy Alexander

2/3 fl oz cream
2/3 fl oz cognac
2/3 fl oz tia maria
nutmeg

Shake cream and liqueurs with crushed ice.
To serve, strain into glasses and sprinkle with nutmeg.
Note: This cocktail is delicious served with coffee after
dinner.

After Dinner

Serves 3 — 4

4 fl oz Calvados
4 fl oz port
2 fl oz orange juice
1 teaspoon orange bitters

Stir in mixing glass and pour into large cocktail glasses.
Note: Calvados, or applejack as it is often known, is an
apple brandy.

Chocapple

2/3 fl oz apple brandy
2/3 fl oz crème de cacao
2/3 fl oz cream
1 teaspoon grenadine

Shake with crushed ice and strain into large cocktail glass or
small tumbler.

Tom Collins

2 fl oz gin
1 teaspoon sugar
juice of small lemon
crushed ice
soda water

Spoon crushed ice into a tall glass. Mix in gin with sugar
and lemon juice.

Hot Drinks

Hot drinks have unique properties: the warmth enhances the flavour, produces a full aroma, and is soothing to the taste.

Hot beverages, alcoholic or non-alcoholic, quickly warm the coldest body, right to the extremities of hands and feet. For this reason, mulled wines and spiced, rum-laced teas invented in the ski countries of Europe are popular with all winter sportsmen.

Hot creamy chocolate is another popular after-snow reviver. And there are several recipes here for delicious after-dinner coffees.

Heated alcohol is quickly absorbed into the bloodstream. Thus the sleep-inducing effect of the liquor is intensified by its warmth. Hot milk is another late night favourite; sweetened and flavoured it is both delicious and beneficial to the insomniac.

For victims of colds and flu, hot honey, lemon or rum, or a combination of all three, is an unbeatable remedy.

This chapter contains recipes for everyone: the sportsman, the restless sleeper, the cold sufferer, and the 'everyman' who just wants to enjoy a cosy nightcap.

Apple Flame

Apple Flame

Serves 10

8 fl oz calvados or apple brandy (applejack)
2 tablespoons Angostura bitters
2 pints boiling water
12 whole cloves
2 fl oz calvados to flame

Pare rind from lemons in half inch strips, including as little of the pith as possible. Squeeze lemons.
Put calvados, bitters, boiling water, cloves and lemon rind and juice together in a pot over a low flame. The mixture should not boil.
Carefully pour reserved calvados over the back of a spoon so that it floats.
Light floating liquor and serve immediately in mugs.

Hot Minted Lemonade

Serves 8 — 10

pared rind of 2 lemons
8 oz sugar
2 pints boiling water
juice of 6 lemons (12-15 fl oz juice)
1 handful crushed or bruised mint leaves
slices of lemon to garnish

Simmer sugar, water and lemon rind for 5 minutes.
Thoroughly mix lemon juice and mint in a heat resistant container.
Pour boiling syrup over lemon and mint.
Serve in heavy glasses or mugs, garnished with slices of lemon.

Black Stripe

2 teaspoons molasses
2 fl oz dark rum
twist lemon peel
boiling water

Put rum, molasses and lemon peel into a heavy mug.
Fill with boiling water, stir and serve.

Sweet Cider

Serves 6

1 large bottle apple cider
3 oz sugar
pinch salt
2 cinnamon sticks
12 cloves
4 fl oz brandy

Place cider, sugar, salt and spices in a large saucepan.
Allow to come to the boil, then take from heat and allow to
cool.
Stand at least 2 hours.
Add brandy, bring back to simmering point, and serve in
small mugs.

Whisky Port

Serves 8

8 fl oz port
13 fl oz Scotch whisky
4 fl oz Drambuie
1 pint freshly brewed tea
3 oz sugar
juice of one lemon

Combine all ingredients in a saucepan over a low flame.
Bring to boiling point and serve immediately in mugs.

Glühwein

Serves 20

3 bottles dry red wine
½ bottle brandy
½ pint water
½ pint orange juice
juice of 2 lemons
thinly pared rind of 1 lemon and 1 orange
6 sticks cinnamon bark
1 orange stuck with 24 cloves.

Combine all ingredients in a large pot and simmer over a low flame. Serve in mugs.
Note: There are many varieties of glühwein. Essentially it is any spiced, mulled red wine.

Gin Mint

2 fl oz gin
½ oz sugar
juice of half lemon
3 fl oz water
mint sprigs

Mix gin and mint, crushing mint thoroughly.
Bring water, lemon juice and sugar to the boil, stirring till sugar is dissolved.
Pour hot lemon onto gin mint, stir and serve.

Oranges and Lemons

Serves 4 — 5

1 orange stuck with 12 cloves
1 pint water
2 tablespoons honey
½ pint orange juice
6 fl oz fresh lemon juice
½ teaspoon cinnamon
pinch allspice
twists of lemon peel to garnish

Simmer orange stuck with cloves in water with honey.
Remove from heat, add orange juice, lemon juice and spices.
Return to heat and allow to warm until steaming, but not
simmering.
Serve in mugs with a twist of lemon peel.

Port Cup

1 bottle port
3 lemons
2 oz castor sugar
8 fl oz water
pimento
cloves

Stick 1 lemon with cloves. Bring water to boil in a heavy
based saucepan, add pimento and boil for a few minutes
further.
Add port, lemon stuck with cloves, lemon juice from two
remaining lemons.
Stir mixture thoroughly, ensuring it simmers as you do so
and serve as required.

Irish Coffee

Serves 4

4 lumps sugar
6 fl oz Irish whisky
½ pint strong boiling coffee
cream

Put 1 lump sugar in each of 4 stemmed heat-proof glasses,
5-7 fl oz capacity.
Pour whisky over sugar, add hot coffee.
Float cream by pouring onto hot coffee over the back of a
spoon

Bullshot

½ pint beef bouillon
6 fl oz vodka
3 tablespoons lemon juice
1½ tablespoons Worcestershire sauce
Tabasco sauce to taste

Heat beef bouillon to near boiling point. Pour into two mugs
and mix in vodka, lemon juice, Worcestershire sauce and
Tabasco, if desired.
This drink can also be served cold over ice cubes.

Café Brûlot

Serves 6

6 lumps sugar
8 fl oz cognac
6 cloves
4 twists orange peel
2 twists lemon peel
1 vanilla bean
2 sticks cinnamon bark
18 fl oz boiling coffee

Heat sugar, spices, vanilla and peels with cognac over low flame
until well warmed. Add hot coffee and ignite.
Serve as soon as flame dies.

Jäger Tee (Hunter's Tea)

Serves 8

1½ pints hot tea (medium strength)
1 pint brandy or rum
juice of 2 lemons
5 tablespoons molasses
¼ teaspoon nutmeg
¼ teaspoon allspice

Mix tea, rum or brandy, lemon juice, molasses and spices in a
pot over a low flame until almost simmering.
Serve steaming in mugs.

Rum Coffee

1 fl oz rum
1 lump sugar
4 fl oz strong black coffee
1 slice lemon

Pour rum over sugar in a large coffee cup or small mug.
Fill with coffee and decorate with a slice of lemon.

Hot Buttered Rum

Serves 1

1 teaspoon melted butter
1 teaspoon brown sugar
2 pinches cinnamon
2 fl oz boiling water
2 fl oz dark rum

Mix melted butter, sugar and cinnamon in the bottom of a mug.
Add water and rum, stir well.

Beer Nightcap

Serves 4

1 pint beer
3 tablespoons honey
1 stick cinnamon
1 pinch nutmeg
1 pinch ground ginger
1 cardamon pod
6 cloves
4 fl oz medium dry sherry

Bring beer and honey to the boil, and simmer gently for 2-3 minutes.
Wrap spices together in a piece of muslin or other fine cloth and tie tightly so that they will not escape.
Drop spice sac into hot beer and leave to soak overnight.
Before serving, add sherry, bring to boiling point and remove spice sac.

Hot Milk Punch

Serves 4

1 pint milk
2 oz sugar
4 fl oz orange juice
4 fl oz grand marnier
2 dashes orange bitters
ground nutmeg and cloves

Bring milk and sugar to the boil, stirring all the time, and take from heat.
Mix orange juice, liqueur and bitters; divide between 4 mugs, and fill each mug with sweetened scalding milk.
Sprinkle each mug with mixed ground nutmeg and cloves.

Hot Froth

Serves 4

1 pint milk
3 egg yolks (lightly beaten)
4 oz sugar
½ teaspoon cinnamon
dash Angostura bitters
dash orange bitters
4 fl oz rum (optional)

Bring milk almost to boil.
Take from heat, add egg yolks and beat well.
Add sugar, cinnamon and bitters and beat again. Add rum if
required.
Serve in mugs.

Hot Brandied Milk

½ pint milk
1 fl oz brandy
cinnamon

Bring milk almost to boiling point. Add brandy and whisk
briskly until brandied milk is frothy.
Dust with cinnamon and serve in mugs.

Vanilla Coffee

Serves 6

3 oz medium ground coffee
1 pint cold water
2 oz sugar
1 vanilla bean
lightly whipped cream

Place coffee, water, sugar and vanilla bean in a saucepan and
very gently heat to boiling point.
Cover and allow mixture to stand five minutes keeping hot,
but not allowing to boil.
Pour into cups and top with a generous swirl of whipped
cream.

Hot Toddy

Serves 2

2 lemons
1 tablespoon honey
6 fl oz water
4 fl oz dark rum

Thinly pare skin from 2 lemons.
Simmer lemon peel with honey and water for five minutes.
Warm rum in a small saucepan. Strain lemon honey into rum, mix and serve in small mugs.

Hot Rum Chocolate

1½ oz cooking chocolate
3 teaspoons sugar
1 fl oz rum
1 pint milk
whipped cream

Melt chocolate in a heavy based saucepan and when melted add rum and sugar.
Stir thoroughly until sugar has dissolved; then slowly add milk and continue to stir until chocolate/rum mixture has combined evenly.
Pour into warmed mugs and pile whipped cream on top.

Mariners Toddy

1 fl oz dark rum
1 teaspoon sugar
3 whole cloves
1 inch cinnamon stick
juice of one lemon

Mix all ingredients together in a warmed mug.
Fill with boiling water, stir once more and serve.

Fireside

2 fl oz marsala
1 fl oz curacao
2 teaspoons honey
3 teaspoons lemon juice
1 egg yolk

Mix egg yolk, and honey together in a heavy based
saucepan.
Add marsala, curacao, honey and lemon juice and heat to simmering
point.
Serve in warmed mugs.

Children's Party Drinks

Drinks to serve at a children's party should be bright and colourful, presented with imagination, thirst quenching and refreshing.

Young children will be delighted by 'boats' or other novelties floating in bowls or glasses. Or you may like to decorate your party table according to some theme; perhaps a punch bowl 'pond' with floating flowers, 'duckling' meringues, and a birthday cake made in a 'duck' mould.

It is a good idea to have jugs of iced milk and fruit juices for children who do not enjoy mixed drinks.

Older children will prefer drinks that are not so sweet: tomato juice cocktails, ginger beer, apple cider, fresh fruit juices and home-made lemonade may be served. Mixed fruit juices, such as pineapple and orange, or apricot and lemon, are popular.

The last recipe in this chapter is a wine cup that would be suitable for young teenagers.

Banana Boat

Serves 10

5 bananas
juice of 1 lemon
½ pint banana syrup
1 pint ice cream
3 pints milk

Cut bananas in half. Trim a slice lengthwise from each half
banana so that you make 10 'boats', curved on the underside
and flat on top. Pour lemon juice over the cut banana to stop
it going brown. Make a 1 inch square paper 'sail', securing it
on a toothpick.
Beat, blend or shake milk with syrup and ice cream.
Pour milkshake into wide glasses, and float a banana boat
in each.

Iceberg

Serves 16

3 oz sugar
8 fl oz water
juice of 6 lemons
2 teaspoons blue vegetable colouring agent
4 large bottles carbonated lemonade
1 large block ice
small plastic boats to decorate

Dissolve sugar by boiling with water. Pour into large punch
bowl. Add lemon juice and blue colouring.
Place large block of ice in bowl to resemble iceberg, pour
lemonade over the ice, and float small plastic boats, one for
each child, on top of the blue drink.
Variation: To make a green sea, substitute carbonated lime
drink for lemonade and colouring.

Fresh Lemon Drink

Serves 6—8

3 large lemons
4 oz of sugar
2 pints boiling water
3 sprigs of mint
2 cups cracked ice
4 slices lemon

Wash whole lemons, then cut into ½ inch cubes, taking care not to lose juice.
Put into a large stoneware jug, add sugar, and pour on boiling water.
Leave approximately 20 minutes, then strain.
Add mint, slices of fresh lemon and ice to lemon drink.
Allow ice to cool drink, then serve.

Chocolate Mint Shake

Serves 6

2 pints milk
½ pint ice cream
4 fl oz chocolate syrup
2 fl oz peppermint syrup
grated chocolate to decorate

Shake or blend milk, ice cream and syrup.
Pour into glasses and decorate with grated chocolate.

Cider Float

Serves 6

1 pint apple juice
2 large bottles sweet or dry apple cider
2 large apples finely chopped
firm pitted cherries and slices of orange to decorate
cracked ice

Mix juice, cider and chopped apple in a jug.
Pour into glasses and decorate with cherries and orange slices.
Add ice to each glass.

Pink Shake

Serves 6

1¾ pints milk
4 scoops ice cream
1 tin raspberries in syrup

Strain tinned fruit into bowl. Reserve fruit.
Add milk and ice cream to syrup.
Beat well, or if you have an electric blender, mix ingredients
in that.
Pour into tall glasses, top with a spoonful of reserved fruit.
Serve with long-handled parfait spoons.

Wine Cup

Serves 24

2 pints orange juice
2 pints peach juice
2 large bottles dry ginger ale
2 bottles dry white wine
1 large block ice
slices of peach and orange to garnish

Mix juices, ginger ale and wine in a punch bowl.
Add a large block of ice.
Decorate with slices of fresh peach and slices of orange.

Ginger Fizz

Serves 6

2 large bottles ginger beer
6 scoops ice cream

Put a scoop of ice cream into each tall glass.
Fill with ginger beer and serve with a long-handled spoon.

Fruit Cup

Serves approximately 36

1 bottle orange cordial
4 large bottles lemonade
4 large bottles dry ginger ale
2 pints pineapple juice
½ pint lemon juice
pulp of 10 passionfruit
2 lb chopped fresh fruit; peaches, pears, apricots, apples,
    bananas, berries, pineapple
6 cups crushed ice

Mix all ingredients in a large punch bowl.

Orange Juice Fizz

Serves 10

2 pints freshly squeezed orange juice
1 large bottle lemonade
fingers of pineapple to decorate
ice cubes

Mix orange juice and lemonade.
Pour into glasses with a finger of pineapple and an ice cube
in each.

Melon Surprise

Serves approximately 30

1 large watermelon
1 cantaloupe melon
½ large pineapple
2 large bottles carbonated lemon drink
2 pints pineapple juice
2 pints orange juice
2 pints ginger ale
4 cups cracked ice

Cut water melon lengthwise, about one-third down.
Scoop out flesh with a melon baller. Scoop cantaloupe melon flesh
with baller and peel and dice pineapple.
Mix melon balls and pineapple cubes in a large (12 pint
capacity) container.
Add carbonated lemon, dry ginger, juices and ice.
Mix well.
Remove any flesh remaining in melon shell, and support it
firmly so that it is level.
Fill hollow melon shell with drink for serving, and refill as
required.
Decorate with flowers if desired.

Pink Lemonade

Serves 8

juice of 4 lemons
2 large bottles lemonade
4 fl oz raspberry syrup
ice cubes
fresh berry fruit to decorate

Mix juice, lemonade and syrup in a jug.
Place an ice cube in each glass.
Fill with pink lemonade and decorate with fresh berries.

Long, Cool Drinks Non-Alcoholic

Too often the 'non-drinker' is faced with the dullest refreshment: plain canned juices, bottled soft drinks or lukewarm watery cordials.

This is quite unnecessary, as the range of non-alcoholic liquid ingredients is considerable, and with a little imagination, decorative and delicious drinks can be created for every occasion.

This chapter contains recipes for milk, fruit, vegetable, tea, coffee and soft drink based beverages.

As with all mixed drinks, chilled utensils and ingredients, careful preparation, and thoughtful use of garnishes makes all the difference. It is easy to make an ordinary thirst-quencher, but with just a little extra effort, every drink that you serve will be a sparkling taste sensation.

Tea Punch

Tea Punch

Serves 15

½ pint peach juice
2 pints orange juice
1 pint strong hot tea
2 teaspoons orange bitters
2 large bottles dry ginger ale
orange slices to garnish

Pour fruit juices and tea over a large block of ice in a punch
bowl.
Add orange bitters and dry ginger ale.
Garnish with slices of orange.

Apricot Froth

4 fl oz apricot juice or nectar
2½ apricots, stewed or canned
scoop ice cream
soda water
nutmeg

Put ice cream in a very tall glass.
Add apricot nectar and fill with soda.
Sprinkle with nutmeg and top with apricot halves.
Serve with a long-handled spoon.

Iced Lemon Tea

6 fl oz tea per person
1-2 teaspoons sugar
1 tablespoon boiling water
juice half lemon.

Brew quantity of tea required, and pour from leaves as soon
as tea is strong enough.
Chill tea in refrigerator.
In each glass dissolve sugar in boiling water.
Add lemon juice and an ice block.
Fill glass with cold tea.
Mix well and serve

Grapefruit Tonic

4 fl oz unsweetened grapefruit juice
tonic (quinine) water
ice cube

Put juice with ice cube in a tall glass.
Fill with tonic water and serve.

Orange Pawpaw

Serves approx. 24

1 x 2 lb fully ripe papaw
1 pint unsweetened pineapple juice
2 pints fresh or unsweetened orange juice
2 large bottles lemonade
2 oranges sliced, to garnish

Peel papaw, cut into cubes, and push through a wire mesh strainer.
Alternatively, liquidize in an electric blender.
Put papaw liquid in a large punch bowl.
Add juices and a large block of ice.
Add lemonade and garnish with orange slices.
Note: Unless you use a liquidizer, it will be necessary to select a particularly ripe papaw.

Peppermint Tea

Serves 4

1 dessertspoon peppermint tea leaves
1 pint water
2 tablespoons honey
1 cup crushed ice

Boil water and brew tea.
Allow to stand about 10 minutes, then pour water off leaves.
Add honey and allow to cool.
Add crushed ice before serving.
Note: Peppermint tea is available in some continental delicatessen, and in health food stores.

Fruit Froth

Serves 2

6 fl oz black cherry juice
6 fl oz pineapple juice
2 fl oz lemon juice
1 egg white
1 cup crushed ice
whole stewed black cherries to decorate

Shake juices and egg white well with ice.
Strain into two tall glasses.
Decorate with cherries.

Party Special

Serves approx. 36

1 bottle lemon squash
juice of 6 lemons
2 fl oz grenadine
1 pint water
6 apples
12 cloves
1 teaspoon nutmeg
2 sticks cinnamon
soda water

Mix lemon squash, lemon juice and grenadine in a large
punch bowl.
Add a large block of ice.
Simmer apples and spices in water until pulpy. Sieve or
liquidize apple.
Allow apple to cool and add to lemon mixture.
Add soda to punch bowl to taste; 6–8 pints should be
sufficient.

Raspberry Punch

1 lb raspberries
½ lb redcurrants
1 lb castor sugar
2½ pints cold water

Thoroughly clean the fruit and rinse in cool, running water.
Puree fruit in blender or push through fine sieve with a
wooden spoon.
Place fruit in a heavy based saucepan with ½ pint water and
½ lb sugar. Gently bring fruit to boiling point, stirring
occasionally.
Strain fruit through fine sieve again and leave to stand.
Combine remaining sugar and water in a saucepan and bring
to boiling point and add to puréed fruit. Leave mixture to
cool, then chill for 1 hour and serve.

Tomato & Yoghurt Cocktail

Serves 2

½ pint tomato juice
6 fl oz natural yoghurt
1 teaspoon finely chopped parsley
1 teaspoon Worcestershire sauce
2 teaspoons lemon juice
freshly ground black pepper

Mix all ingredients together and pour into tall glasses.

Creamy Applenut

Serves 4

½ pint unsweetened apple juice
½ pint sweet cider
1 dessertspoon honey
4 tablespoons ice cream
finely chopped almonds and grated nutmeg to decorate

Thoroughly shake apple juice with honey and crushed ice.
Strain and divide equally between four glasses.
Add spoon of ice cream to each glass, and fill with cider,
stirring with long-handled spoon.
Top with sprinkle of nutmeg and chopped nuts. Serve with
spoon.

Fruit Punch

Serves 12 — 14

4 apples
4 tablespoons honey
6 cloves
2 sticks cinnamon bark
1 pint water
1 pint pineapple juice
1 pint orange juice
1 pint soda water
seedless grapes, mint and ice cubes to garnish

Peel and slice apples.
Simmer with honey, water and spices until pulpy. Strain and
chill liquid.
Mix apple liquid and fruit juices in a large bowl or jug.
Add soda.
Garnish with grapes (about 4 oz) and mint leaves and top
with ice cubes.

Summer Tea

Serves approx. 20

2 pints fragrant China tea
2 pints orange juice
1 pint apple juice
1 pint white grape juice
½ tablespoon angostura bitters
mint sprigs, berries and orange slices to garnish
soda water

Mix tea, juices and bitters in a large punch bowl.
Add a large block of ice.
Garnish with mint, berries and orange slices.
Serve in tall glasses, with soda added to taste.

Pineapple Ginger

pineapple juice
dry ginger ale
ground ginger
gardenias or ginger flowers to decorate

Mix equal quantities dry ginger ale and pineapple juice.
Add an ice cube and sprinkle with ground ginger.
If desired, float a gardenia or ginger flower in drink, and
serve with a straw.

Orangeade

Juice of 8 oranges
thinly pared rind of 2 oranges
1 quart water
4 oz sugar
crushed ice

Place orange rind and sugar in ½ pint of water and simmer
gently until all sugar has dissolved (about 15-20 minutes).
Leave to cool.
Pour orange juice and remaining 1½ pints water into a jug.
Thoroughly mix this, then stir in cooled syrup and
crushed ice.

Passionfruit Banana

Serves 6

4 oz sugar
4 fl oz water
4 bananas
juice of 2 lemons
¾ pint passionfruit pulp
soda water
2 cups crushed ice

Boil sugar and water. Cool.
Slice bananas. Pour lemon juice over bananas.
Put passionfruit pulp, sliced bananas and sugar syrup in a large
jug and mix well.
Add crushed ice and soda water to taste.
Note: If fresh passionfruit is unavailable, use canned pulp and
omit sugar syrup from recipe.

Tiger Shake

1 pint chilled milk
1 banana, mashed
2 teaspoons malt
2 teaspoons honey
1 egg, beaten

Mix banana, malt and honey together in a mixing bowl.
Slowly add beaten egg and finally add milk.
Serve in tall glasses with parfait spoons.

Tomato Juice Cocktail

4–6 fl oz tomato juice
juice of half a lemon
dash of Worcestershire sauce
freshly ground pepper
crushed ice
slice lemon to garnish

Shake tomato and lemon juice, Worcestershire sauce and
pepper with ice.
Strain into glass.
Garnish with slice of lemon.

Lemon Spice

Serves 8

rind of one lemon and one orange cut into strips
6 cloves
2 sticks cinnamon
2 cardamom pods (optional)
½ lb sugar
2 pints water
juice of 6-8 lemons

Boil sugar, spices and peel with water for 5 minutes.
Take from heat, add lemon juice, and allow to stand overnight.
Strain.
Serve poured over ice cubes.

White Gold

Serves approx. 20

15 fl oz unsweetened grapefruit juice
1 pint unsweetened pineapple juice
2 pints strong hot tea
2 large bottles dry ginger ale
1 small tin grapefruit segments
fresh pineapple cubes to decorate
1 large block ice

Mix tea and fruit juices in punch bowl.
Add large block of ice.
Pour in dry ginger ale, and add pineapple cubes and grapefruit segments with juice.

Lemon Fizz

¼ pint natural yoghurt
1 tablespoon lemon juice
1 x ½ pint bottle bitter lemon

Mix all ingredients together and serve in tall glasses.

Orange Egg Flip

Juice of 3 oranges
1 teaspoon honey
1 egg, beaten

Combine honey with orange juice and gradually beat in egg.
Serve immediately in a tall glass.

Appleade

Serves 6—8

4 large apples, peeled and sliced
2 pints water
5 tablespoons honey
2 sticks cinnamon
8 cloves
½ teaspoon ground ginger
pinch coriander
soda water

Boil sliced apple, honey and spices with water till mushy.
Mash well, then put through a strainer; or blend cooked apple
in a liquidiser.
Half-fill glasses with apple liquid, add a spoonful of crushed
ice and fill with soda.
Stir well and serve.

Cola Cloud

5 fl oz coca cola
3 fl oz milk
2 ice cubes

Place ice cubes in a ½ pint glass.
Add coca cola and milk, mix and serve.

Raspberry Fix

Serves 6

4 fl oz raspberry syrup
1 pint soda water
2 pints semi-sweet apple cider
juice of 2 lemons
½ teaspoon cinnamon
2 cups crushed ice

Mix syrup, lemon juice, soda and cider in a large jug.
Add crushed ice and cinnamon.
Stir well and serve.

Cool Mix

1 lump sugar
2 dashes orange bitters
1 teaspoon lemon juice
1 long twist lemon peel
1 strip cucumber peel
soda water

Put sugar in tall glass, splash with bitters.
Add lemon juice, an ice cube and lemon and cucumber peel.
Fill with soda.

Mint Cooler

Serves 6

4 oz sugar
4 fl oz water
handful of mint leaves
juice of 4 lemons
1 pint unsweetened pineapple juice
2 cups crushed ice
soda water

Boil sugar and water till dissolved. Cool.
Put mint into cooled syrup and crush with the back of a
spoon.
Allow to stand overnight and strain.
Add lemon and pineapple juice to mint syrup. Mix well.
Add crushed ice and soda water to taste. Serve.

Passionfruit Nectar

Serves 10

pulp of 10 passionfruit and
4 oz sugar syrup
OR 12 oz canned passionfruit pulp
15 fl oz peach juice
4 dashes orange bitters
juice of 2 lemons
1 pint soda
peach slices to garnish

Mix all ingredients in a punch bowl.
Add a large block of ice.
Garnish with fresh peach slices.

Limeade

Serves 8—10

6 oz sugar
6 fl oz water
juice of 10 limes
2 pints water
mint sprigs and twists of lime peel to garnish

Boil sugar and water till dissolved.
Mix sugar syrup, lime juice and water in large jug.
Add ice cubes and garnish with mint and peel.

Grape Cup

Serves 8—10

1 pint white grape juice
juice of two lemons
½ pint unsweetened pineapple juice
1 large bottle dry ginger ale
fresh pineapple cubes and seedless green grapes to garnish
2 cups crushed ice

Mix juices with dry ginger in a large jug.
Add crushed ice and garnish with fresh pineapple cubes and
seedless grapes.

Tropic Fluff

Serves 4

½ pint unsweetened pineapple juice
1 x 10 oz can mango slices, **OR**
flesh of two mangoes and 2 oz sugar
juice of one lemon
white of one egg

Blend all ingredients thoroughly in a liquidizer.
Serve in tumblers.
Note: 1. If you do not have a liquidizer, push mango through
a strainer, discarding fibrous residue, and whisk with other
ingredients with an egg beater.
          2. If mango is unavailable, substitute ½ pint orange
juice.

Lemon Orange Shake

Serves 4—6

juice of 10 large oranges
juice of 6 lemons
1 tablespoon grenadine
1 dash orange bitters
white of one egg
1 cup crushed ice

Shake all ingredients thoroughly.
Pour unstrained into glasses.

Cool Velvet

small bottle sarsparilla per person
1 scoop ice cream

Place ice cream in glass.
Fill with sarsparilla.
Serve with a long-handled spoon.

Citrus Fizz

½ fl oz lime cordial
4 sprigs mint
juice half a lemon
3 fl oz fresh orange juice
2 dashes orange bitters
ginger ale
slice of orange to garnish

Crush mint with lime cordial.
Add lemon and orange juices, bitters and an ice cube.
Fill with dry ginger ale and garnish with a slice of orange.

Grenadine Grape

Serves 2

½ pint grape juice
1 tablespoon grenadine
1 egg white
soda

Thoroughly shake grape juice, grenadine and egg white with
crushed ice.
Strain into two 8-10 fl oz glasses and fill with soda.

Chocolate Cherry

Serves 2

2 tablespoons cerise (cherry syrup)
1 tablespoon powdered cocoa
15 fl oz milk
crushed ice
canned or fresh black cherries to decorate

Mix cocoa to a paste with cherry syrup.
Add milk and blend.
Shake thoroughly with ice.
Strain into glass and serve garnished with cherries.

Blackcurrant Fizz

1 fl oz blackcurrant syrup
juice of half a lemon
tonic (quinine) water
slice lemon to garnish

Mix syrup and lemon juice in tall (8-10 fl oz) glass.
Fill with tonic water.
Garnish with slice of lemon.

Carrot Crunch

6 fl oz carrot juice
1 tablespoon finely chopped parsley
1 teaspoon finely chopped celery
juice of half a lemon
celery sprig to garnish

Mix carrot juice, parsley, celery and lemon juice.
Add a cube of ice and garnish with a sprig of celery.

Sweet Citrus

Serves 4

½ pint orange juice
1 pint grapefruit juice
1 tablespoon grenadine
¼ teaspoon nutmeg

Shake all ingredients thoroughly with crushed ice.
Pour unstrained into tall glasses.

Eggnog

1 egg
1 tablespoon sugar
6 fl oz milk
½ teaspoon vanilla essence
pinch nutmeg

Beat egg with sugar till frothy.
Add milk and vanilla and beat further.
Pour into glass and sprinkle with nutmeg.

Grenadine Grapefruit

4 fl oz grapefruit juice, canned or fresh
1 tablespoon grenadine
soda
maraschino cherry to garnish

Put an ice cube in an 8-10 fl oz glass.
Add grapefruit juice and grenadine. Mix.
Fill with soda and garnish with a cherry.

Index